A LETTER

BALLANCING THE NECESSITY OF KEEPING A LAND-FORCE IN TIMES OF PEACE WITH THE DANGERS THAT MAY FOLLOW ON IT

by

JOHN SOMERS

Published by *The Rota* at the University of Exeter
1974

Printed in Great Britain by
The Printing Unit at the University of Exeter

Bibliographical Note

A letter, ballancing the necessity of keeping a land-force in times of peace: with the dangers that may follow on it was the government's reply to Trenchard and Moyle's *Argument* against standing armies (previously reprinted by *The Rota*). The author of this tract, which is usually called the *Ballancing letter*, was probably John Somers, the Junto's chief of propaganda as well as Lord Chancellor. His task was to defend the ministry and the king against a new country opposition, composed of old whigs, tories and country gentlemen drawn together by their resentment of the war taxes and by the opportunities presented by the forthcoming parliamentary elections of 1698. The peace of Ryswick was regarded by them as an occasion to relieve their tax burdens while casting out the Junto of whig lords. William saw that stalemate peace as merely a cessation of hostilities—a truce in his life-long struggle against Louis XIV and French domination of Europe, now a frightening possibility if the prospective union of the crowns of France and Spain were to occur on the death of the ailing Charles II of Spain.

The *Ballancing letter* presents the government's case for retaining a land-force (which would not be the standing army forbidden by the Bill of Rights). Such a force would be a deterrent against French invasion, a militia being insufficient against a professional army. The author distinguishes the current situation from the historical examples pressed in the *Argument*; moreover the establishment will be scrutinized yearly by the House of Commons. Thus the alleged dangers of arbitary government are balanced by the necessity of defending English liberties against invasion.

The classic discussion of the standing army controversy is chapter 23 of Macaulay's *History of England*. Various opinions are briefly catalogued in E. A. Miller, 'Some arguments used by English pamphleteers, 1697-1700, concerning a standing army', *Journal of Modern History* 18 (1946), 306-13. Lois G. Schwoerer, 'The literature of the standing army controversy, 1697-1699', *Huntington Library Quarterly* 28 (1965), 187-212 provides a discussion which should be superseded by a full examination in her *'No standing army': The anti-army ideology in seventeenth-century England* (Baltimore, forthcoming). See also J. R. Western, *The English militia in the eighteenth century* (London, 1965) and the treatments of seventeenth and eighteenth-century ideologies cited in the *Bibliographical Note* to Trenchard and Moyle's *Argument*.

The *Ballancing letter* exists in a number of copies, apparently all on the same poor quality paper which has usually become quite brown. No substantial variations in the text have been discovered among the fifteen copies examined although there were press corrections: the spacing of 'ballancing' on p. 1 was changed, a wider space between the paragraphs on p. 2 was introduced and the reversed page number 10 was corrected. This tract was included in *A Collection of State Tracts*, 3 vols (London, 1706).

The *Ballancing letter*, Wing S4642, is reproduced from a copy in Goldsmiths' Library, University of London Library, with the permission of the Director. Goldsmiths' Library printed catalogue, 3469.

A LETTER,

BALLANCING THE

NECESSITY

OF KEEPING

A Land-Force

In Times of

PEACE:

WITH

The DANGERS that may follow on it.

Printed in the Year 1697.

A LETTER,

Ballancing the

NECESSITY OF KEEPING

A Land-Force

In Times of

PEACE.

SIR,

WE have at laſt an Honourable Peace, which was much Longed for by us all, but Deſpaired of by many. *England* is now the Wonder of the World; nothing can hurt us, but Animoſities and Jealouſies among

among our selves. If we maintain the Peace with as much Prudence and Judgment, as we have shewed Spirit and Courage in carrying on the War, we shall give Laws to all about us; and secure that Quiet, which we have procured to the rest of *Europe*.

The Means of doing this, is now the common Subject of Discourse. All agree in one Thing, That we ought to maintain our Empire on the Sea with powerful Fleets, strong Summer and Winter Guards; and that our Stores ought to be well filled, and our great Ships kept in such a State, that we may be in a condition upon short Warning to set out Royal Fleets. This is so necessary, that I suppose it is needless to spend more time upon it. The only Point in which our Opinions may perhaps differ, is, whether we ought to maintain so considerable a Force at Land, as will be sufficient to make a Stand against an Invasion; or whether the Militia can be made so considerable, that we may trust to it at home, as well as to our Fleets abroad, and be safe in this.

I will not suggest so unbecoming a Thought, as to imagine that any of our Neighbours will seek to take Advantages against us, or break the Peace, and invade us contrary to the Honour and Faith of Treaties. No, I will not suspect it. But the best Guaranty of a Peace, is a good Force to maintain it: And the surest way to keep all our Neighbours to an exact Performance of Articles, is to be upon our Guard. They will be then faithful to Agreements; when they see no Opportunities of Surprizing us, and that our Peace does not lay us asleep, and make us forget the Art of War. I mean, it is no Reflection on any of the Neighbouring Princes, when I conclude that their Faith is not so absolute a Security, but that we must help them to be true to their Word, by shewing them that they are not like to gain much by breaking it.

But mistake me not:
When I seem to prepare you to consider the Necessity of keeping a Land-Force, I am far from the Thought of a *Standing Army*. Any Man who would pretend to give a Jealousy of the Nation to the King, and suggest that he could not be safe among them without he were environ'd with Guards and Troops, as it was in the late Reigns, ought to by abhorred by every true *English-man*, by every Man who loves Liberty, and his Country. The Case at present is, Whether considering the Circumstances that we and our Neighbours are now in, it may not be both prudent and necessary for us to keep up a reasonable Force from Year to Year. The State of Affairs both at Home and Abroad being every Year to be considered in Parliament, that so any such Force may be either encreased, lessened, or quite laid aside, as they shall see cause. I will not Argue with you so unfairly, as to urge much the Rea-

sons that we have of Trusting the King; for how much soever may be said on this Head, either from his Temper, his Circumstances, his Interest, and the Course of his past Life, either with Relation to the United Provinces, or to us here in *England*, and with how much Reason soever this might be prosecuted, yet I will not lay much Weight on it; for it is not just to press an Argument that puts another Man in Pain, when he goes to answer it: I know it may be said, That Men are but Men; so that we make a dangerous Experiment of their Virtue, when we put too much in their Power: And that what is done to one King, who deserves it, and will manage it faithfully, will be made an Argument to do the same for another King, that has neither Merit nor Capacity to entitle him to so entire a Confidence.

To say all in one Word, if we were in the same Condition in which we and our Neighbours were an Age ago, I should reject the Proposition with Horrour. But the Case is altered; the whole World, more particularly our Neighbours, have now got into the mistaken Notion of keeping up a mighty Force; and the powerfullest of all these happens to be our next Neighbour, who will very probably keep up great Armies: And we may appear too Inviting, if we are in such an open and unguarded Condition, that the Success of the Attempt may seem to be not only probable, but certain. *England* is an open Country, full of Plenty, every where able to Subsist an

Ar-

Army: Our Towns and Cities are all open; our Rivers are all fordable; no Passes nor strong Places can stop an Enemy, that should Land upon us. So that the whole Nation lies open to any Army that should once come into it. To this you may reply, Can an Army be brought together, with a Fleet to bring it over, and we know nothing of it? These Things require time, and we cannot be supposed so destitute of Intelligence as not to know of such Preparations. In such a case, our Fleet will cover us, while our Militia may be exercised, and marched where the Danger is apprehended. This may seem plausible, and will no doubt work on such as do not consider Things with the Attention that is necessary. But do not we remember, that we were lately twice almost surprized; once from *La Hogue*, and again from *Calais*. We must not expect that God will always work Miracles for us, if we are wanting to our selves. If in a time of War and Jealousy we were so near the being fatally overrun, without either Warning or Intelligence; it is much more possible to see such Designs laid in a time of Sloth and Quiet, when we are under no Fears nor Apprehensions: And this may be so managed, that the Notice we may have of it, may come too late for us to be able to prevent or resist it. And what will our Intelligence signify, if we are in no condition either to hinder the Descent, or to withstand the Force that may be sent against us. Absolute Governments, where

all

all depends on the Will of the Prince, and where Men are ruined, who fail either in performing what is expected from them, or in keeping the Secrefy that is enjoyned them, can both contrive and execute Things in another manner, than can be conceived by thofe who have the Happinefs to live in free Governments. Troops may have fuch Orders for Marches and Counter-marches, that thofe who are on the Place fhall not be able to judge what is intended, till it is not poffible to hinder it. Crofs Winds may make this come yet later, to thofe who have a Sea between them. Orders may be given to many different Perfons in many different Places, who fhall know nothing of one another, till they meet in a General Rendezvous.

It is true, we muft fuppofe that we fhall have good Fleets abroad, but one would not put fo great a thing, as the Safety of the Nation, to fuch a Hazard, nor depend upon a fingle Security when that is liable to Accidents. The fame Wind that may bring over a Fleet, and Army, to invade us, may keep our Ships in Port; fo that it fhall not be poffible for them to look out, or if they fhould have a favourable Minute to get out, it may fo fhatter them that they fhall not be able to defend either our Seas or our Ports. This may well be fuppofed, for it really happened when the King landed firft in *England*. The late King had then a powerful Fleet, which, if it could have engaged the *Dutch*, would have been probably too hard

for

for them, especially considering the Transport Fleet that they guarded; but the East Wind, that brought over the King, kept them in the River till the *Dutch* had past them; and when they got out, a Storm stop'd and shattered them, so that without being able to come to any Action, they were laid up. And would any Man hazard the Nation upon such a Contingency.

But the last thing in reserve is our *Militia*. Great Bodies may be brought together; The Men are brave, capable of Discipline, and they naturally love their Countrey: Their Officers being Men of Estates, may be well trusted with the Concerns of the Nation, in which they have so good a Stake.

I will never enter upon so invidious an Argument, as to disparage our *Militia*, or derogate from them: I do not doubt but they are much the best in the World, and if they had a Militia to deal with, I should doubt little of the Decision. But you and I have seen Armies too much not to know the difference that is between Troops that have been long trained, who have learned the Art and are accustomed to the Discipline of War, and the best Bodies of raw and undisciplined Multitudes. The whole Method of War is now such, that disciplined Troops must prove a very unequal Match, to much greater Numbers of Men, who yet perhaps, upon half their Practice, might prove too hard for them. I know it will be urged, that our Militia may be so trained and

defied, as to be made more capable of Service then perhaps they are at present: This is a Work of Time; a Project that depends upon so many Particulars, and may be subject to so many Slips in the Execution, that it must be confess'd a Nation is much exposed, if its Safety and Preservation must depend upon such Uncertainties. We have Troops that have pass'd through a long Apprentiship, and to our cost have learned that unhappy Trade, which is now become so universal, that it is thereby made necessary; we must either be preserved by it, or we must perish by it. Many gallant Gentlemen have broke the course of their Studies, and the other Methods of Life they were in: It will not only be a hardship put upon them, but it will be the rendring our selves naked and defencelefs, if, after all the Reputation that we have risen to in War, we should sink into an unbecomming Remisness in Peace, and upon the remote and uncertain Fears of Dangers that will probably never happen, expose our selves to those which we may certainly look for, as soon as we have put our selves out of a Capacity of resisting them. To tell you Truth, I cannot see some Men grow all of the sudden such wonderful Patriots, so jealous of the Prerogative, and such Zealots for publick Liberty, without remembring what their Behaviour was, some years ago, in the late Reigns; when we had not only all the justest Causes of Jealousie, but all the Certainties of Evidence: The Designs were bare-faced, and the Attempts
were

were bold; and yet some were then silent, and others went into them, with as hearty a Zeal for Arbitrariness as they seem now to put on for Liberty. The Methods they have taken during the War have been so ill disguised, that few will believe they are in earnest, when they talk of Liberty and Law, who seemed to have laboured hard to lay us open to Invasion and Conquest. What they could not compass during the War, they hope now to bring about by laying us asleep in Peace; for if we let go a real Security, and trust to an imaginary one, we may pay too dear for the Experiment, and be convinced of our Error when it will be no more in our Power to correct it.

But I know some will urge the *Roman* and *Lacedemonian* States for our Militia. It is a wrong way of arguing, to apply the Precedent of any one Time to another, unless all Things in both Times did agree. Every Thing is safe in any State, when it is equal, if not superior to those about it. *Lacedemon* and *Rome* were at least upon the same foot with their Neighbours. They were indeed far superiour to them: At *Lacedemon* they bred their Youth to nothing but War, or to other Exercises that render them fit for it, and to a short and pointed way of Talking. They had neither Arts nor Learning among them: So that their whole Republick was like a Standing Army, that threatned the rest of *Greece*. The *Romans*, in the Times of their Liberty, were but a little distinguished from them. They allowed indeed of Agriculture, and put their own Hands to it, which the *Lacedemonians* left to their Slaves: But they were all trained to War; and no Man among them could pretend to Imployments, 'till he could reckon up so many Campaigns, and shew the Wounds he had received in them: So that here was a Military Republick. It was not only equal but superior to all about them, for this very thing, and so no wonder if it conquered them. These Precedents can never suit our Times, unless we could change our whole Constitution at home, as well as the State of Affairs abroad, and banish from us not only Luxury but both Wealth and Trade. The accounts that we have of the Militia in *Sweden* are not very encouraging: The new modelling it there has signified little to preserve their Liberty.

Others will perhaps ask, How did our Ancestors not only defend our Countrey, but render it terrible to all about it, particularly to those from whom we seem now to be most in danger? This is a Topick that may furnish a great deal of popular Eloquence, and may impose upon such as are proud of the Valour of their Countrey, and have read only so much History as to remember the Names of some Battels, and the Numbers of the Armies. But all were then alike as to this Matter, while all Nations were equally ignorant of War, and were only set on the Arts of Peace; then, no doubt, in those short Wars that broke out, the braver Nation had always the better. But it

is

is evident from the firſt Beginnings of Hiſtory down to this day, that Regular Troops were always too hard for a Militia. *Lacedemon, Athens,* and *Thebes*, in their Turns had the better of one another, as their Armies were better trained, and had more Experience in War. At laſt the King of *Macedon*, who had been much deſpiſed by them, ſubdued them all. *Cyrus*, by training the *Perſians*, conquered the *Babylonians*; and *Alexander* by the Army which his Father had trained, thô he had numerous Armies, or rather a great Militia brought againſt him, yet he made an eaſy as well as a ſpeedy Conqueſt of the *Perſian* Empire. While the *Romans* were but a Militia, thô they were the beſt that ever was, they made War on their Neighbours, who were weaker than they, with great Advantage; but when *Hanniball* came againſt them with a trained Army, they fell before him upon every Occaſion, till a long War had taught them that Art, and then they not only beat him out of *Italy*, but forced *Carthage* to a Submiſſion. Nothing ſtood before the *Roman* Armies, as long as they were kept under Diſcipline, but when all the order of War was broke, and they became a Militia, the Northern Nations in *Europe*, as well as the Saracens in the *Eaſt*, over-run the *Roman* Empire. As the Saracens ſlackened their Diſcipline, the *Turks* carried it from them: And if they had depended on their *Timariots*, and had not truſted more to their *Janiſaries* and *Spahi's*, they had not been the Terror of *Christendom* for so many Ages. So certain it is, from the Histories of all Nations, that regular and disciplined Troops will be far superior to the best and strongest Militia in the World.

To all this it may be said, How did we do in Queen *Elisabeth*'s Time? Our Militia was then our only Army; to it we trusted, and we were preserved by it. But I must crave leave to put you in mind of some Particulars in this part of our History: We were then in such imminent Danger, that we were given for gone by the wisest Men of the Age: It was the Storms and Winds, the disproportioned Bulk of their Ships, the Stiffness of the Orders, and the Distaste given to the Prince of *Parma*; all which concurred at that time to save *England*: Neither our Militia, nor our Fleet had share in it. There was an extraordinary Concurrence of many Things in that juncture that preserved us: But it were to presume too much on Providence to lay our selves as open as we were then, because we were at that time so wonderfully delivered. But I must tell you our Danger is now much greater: *Spain*, it is true, had then a great Armada, vast Treasures, and well disciplined Armies; But tho' their Army lay near us in *Flanders*, the Scene of their Councils, their Fleet and Treasures were at a great distance from us: And yet all the wise Men of that time thought we must have perished then. The Danger is now both nearer and greater; a mighty Power, well united, and practised in War, and a

great

great Naval Force is in view of us. It will be therefore no Argument, becauſe we run a great risk in Q. *Eliſabeth*'s time, but were wonderfully ſaved, that therefore now, when we may be in greater hazard, and have a more formidable Neighbour at our very Doors, we ought to take no care of our ſelves, but neglect the Only probable means of our Preſervation; we have had Two wonderful Eighty Eights, but we preſume too much if we look for a Third, without taking any further Care how, or by what means, we ſhall be ſaved.

I will add no more on this head, but will only tell you a Saying of one of the *Vere*'s, which is ſtill remembred in the Family. The Queen ſent to the States for thoſe two famous Generals, to command her Army. It ſeemed full of Zeal and Courage; The Queen rid up and down through it, to animate the Soldiers, and was every where anſwered with Shouts and Acclamations: She asked one of the Brothers, what he thought of the Army; he anſwered, It was a brave Army: But ſhe ſaw by his manner that he was in ſome doubt about it, ſo ſhe charged him to explain himſelf; he ſaid, He had not the Name of a Coward in the World, but he was the only Coward there. They were all wiſhing to have the *Spaniards* land, and every Man was telling what Feats he would then do; he was the only Man that was trembling for fear of it.

The

The last and strongest Objection against all this is, That this Force will grow upon us, and continue among us: It will have such an Influence within Doors, that it will maintain it self in the H. of Commons; or, if that should fail, it will turn them out of Doors, and quickly find ways to subsist, to grow upon the Ruins of Liberty and Property. This is a large Field; and History is so full of Instances this way, that it will be easie to open copiously on the subject. From the *Pretorian* Cohorts down to our modern Armies, enough can be gathered to give a very frightful Representation of a Standing Army. Who doubts it? But all the Rhetorick that this head will afford is wrong applied in this case. It is not to be supposed, but that once a year a Parliament must have this matter a-fresh under their Consideration. They will see how the State of Affairs varies, either at Home or Abroad; and whether the Forces are brought under such a Management, that there is just cause of Jealousy. And I leave it to you to judge, whether it is possible in so short a time, so to model and influence it, as to prepare them to invade their Country, and to destroy our Constitution. What *Cesar*, with all his Genius, could not work his Army to, but after Ten Years Conduct and Success, can give small Encouragement to others to attempt to bring it about, in one Year. Perhaps you are more afraid of a Secret Influence, than of Open Violence from them. The short
of

of this is, You are afraid the House will be corrupted: I confess it is hard to answer this, Jealousy is stubborn, and incurable; Melancholy when it grows to be a Disease, raises many imaginary Fears; they who are haunted with that sullen Humour, neither know what they are Afraid of, nor why. Possible Accidents are ever before them; and the thinking of these perpetually, ruines their Health, sours their Humour, and makes them neglect all their present and certain Concerns, while they are ever dreaming of what will probably never happen. We must consider our present Danger, and the likeliest Ways of securing our selves from it, without amusing our selves with what may possibly be brought about at some distance of time. Our Representatives do well to secure our Constitution, by the most effectual Means they can think on: But after all, we must trust *England* to a *House of Commons*, that is to it self. When ever the fatal Time comes, that this Nation grows weary of Liberty, and has neither the Virtue, the Wisdom, nor the Force to preserve its Constitution, it will deliver all up; let all the Laws possible, and all the Bars imaginable, be put in the way to it. It is no more possible to make a Government immortal, than it is to make a Man immortal. I do not deny but several Inconveniences may be apprehended from a Standing Force, and therefore I should not go about to perswade you to it, if the Thing did not seem indispensibly necessary

to

to our Preservation. I would not have us venture upon present and certain Ruine, because that which must preserve us now from it, may at some time hereafter have ill Effects on our Liberty. They cannot be Considerable as long as *England* is true to it self; and whensoever the Nation has lost that Noble Sense of Liberty, by which it has been so long preserved, it will soon make Fetters for it self, tho it should find none at hand ready made.

To conclude, This Matter is of so nice, and yet of so important a Nature, that it ought to be severely examined, without false Colours, or popular Rhetorick; you know me to be so jealous of Liberty, to have been always so true to it, to have ventured so much for it, and to have such a Stake in it, that you cannot suspect me. You know that I neither have, nor can have any Views in this Matter, but at our present Safety, as well as the Continuance of our Constitution and Liberty for the future.